Learning Is Fun!

KATHY ROSS
C·R·A·F·T·S
LETTER
SOUNDS

by Kathy Ross

Illustrated by Jan Barger

The Millbrook Press
Brookfield, Connecticut

To Cindi,
who is doing a wonderful job carrying on!
Thank you!—KR

Library of Congress Cataloging-in-Publication Data
Ross, Kathy (Katharine Reynolds), 1948-
Kathy Ross crafts letter sounds / Kathy Ross ; illustrated by Jan Barger.
p. cm. — (Learning is fun!)
ISBN 0-7613-2102-0 (lib. bdg.) 0-7613-1491-1 (pbk.)
1. Handicraft—Juvenile literature. 2. Alphabet—Juvenile literature.
[1. Handicraft. 2. Alphabet.] I. Barger, Jan, 1948- ill. II. Title. III. Learning is fun!
(Brookfield, Conn.)
TT160 .R714234 2002
745.5—dc21   [[E]]   2001030120

Published by The Millbrook Press, Inc.
2 Old New Milford Road
Brookfield, Connecticut 06804
www.millbrookpress.com

Printed in the United States of America
(lib)   5 4 3 2 1
(pbk)   5 4 3

Table of Contents

KATHY ROSS C•R•A•F•T•S
LETTER SOUNDS

Aa is for ...

Activity on an Anthill

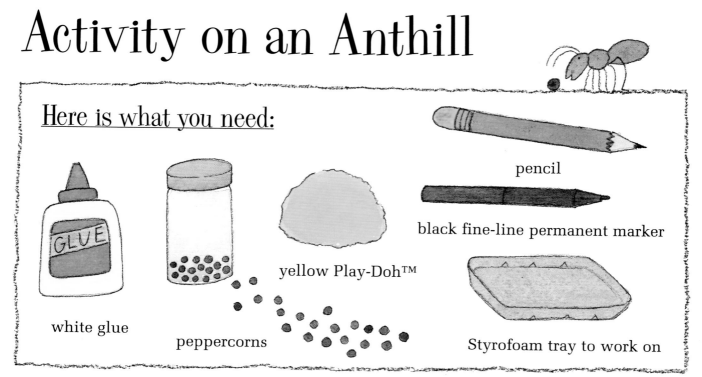

Here is what you need:

white glue

peppercorns

yellow Play-Doh™

pencil

black fine-line permanent marker

Styrofoam tray to work on

Here is what you do:

1. Working on the Styrofoam tray, shape a handful of Play-Doh™ into a cone-shaped hill. Use the pencil to poke a hole in the top of the cone.

2. Use three peppercorns to make each ant. Dip the peppercorns in glue, then press them into the sides of the anthill to look like ants that are crawling up and down the hill.

3. Use the marker to draw three legs on each side of the middle peppercorn of each ant's body.

4. Let the Play-Doh™ dry hard on the Styrofoam tray.

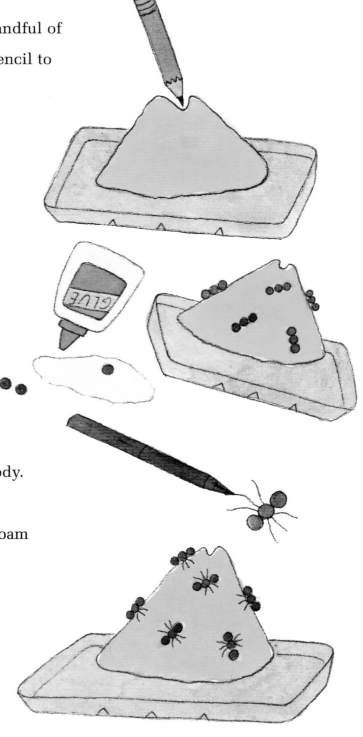

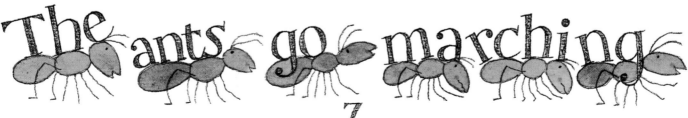

Bb is for . . .

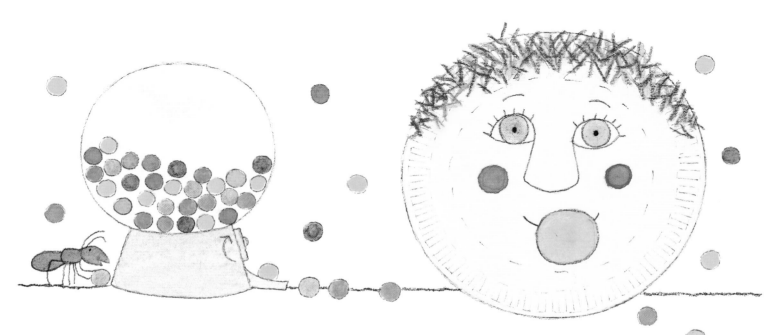

Bubble-Blowing Boy

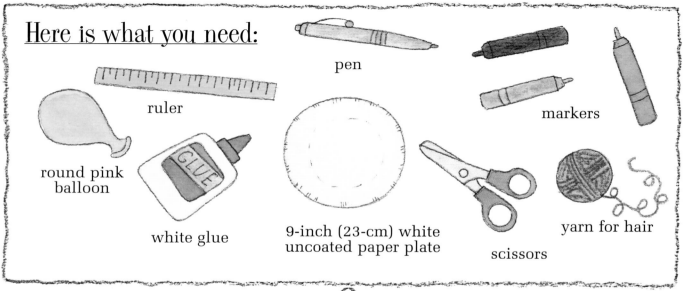

Here is what you need:

pen

ruler

markers

round pink balloon

white glue

9-inch (23-cm) white uncoated paper plate

scissors

yarn for hair

Here is what you do:

1. Use the markers to draw a face on the eating side of the plate.

2. Cut yarn for hair. Glue the yarn hair to the top of the plate face.

3. Use the pen to poke a small hole through the mouth of the face. Blow up the pink balloon to about 4 inches (10 cm) across. Tie the end of the balloon in a knot. Slip the knot of the balloon through the front of the hole in the mouth to secure it. It will look like a very big bubble-gum bubble.

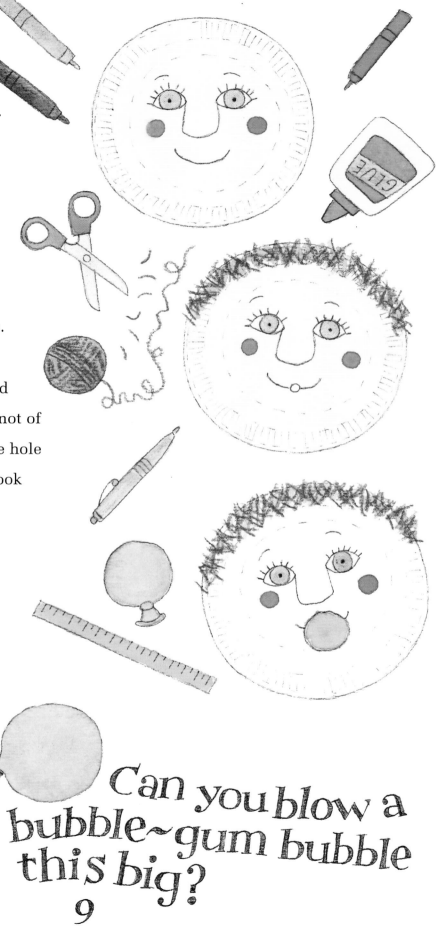

Can you blow a bubble~gum bubble this big?

Cc is for . . .

Creepy, Crawly Caterpillar

Here is what you need:

ruler

two tiny wiggle eyes

Styrofoam packing worm

two map pins

Styrofoam tray to work on

scissors

yellow and green construction paper

green glitter

white glue

hole punch

Here is what you do:

1. To make the body of the caterpillar, cover the packing worm with glue, then sprinkle it with green glitter. Let the project dry on the Styrofoam tray.

2. The tipped-up end of the packing worm will be the head of the caterpillar. Glue the two wiggle eyes to the front of the head. Push the two map pins partway into the head above the eyes for the antennae.

3. Punch two holes from the yellow paper. Glue them to the back of the caterpillar for spots.

4. Cut a 4-inch (10-cm) leaf shape from the green paper. Glue the caterpillar to the center of the leaf. Use the hole punch to "munch" some nibbles out of one side of the leaf.

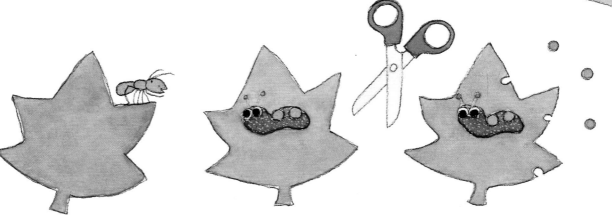

Don't let him crawl away!

Dd is for . . .

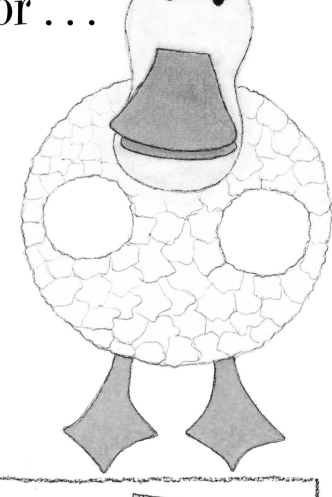

Downy Duck

Here is what you need:

newspaper
to work on

9-inch (23-cm)
white paper plate

scissors

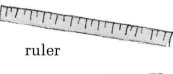

white glue

ruler

four white tissues

orange, white, and black
construction paper

Here is what you do:

1. Cut a hole on each side of the middle of the paper plate just big enough for your hand to fit through—2 to 3 inches (5 to 8 cm) wide. Your hands will form the wings of the duck.

2. Tear the tissues into 1-inch (2.5-cm) pieces. Glue the tissue pieces all over the bottom of the plate for feathers.

3. Cut a head and neck for the duck from the white construction paper. Glue the neck to the plate above the wings so that the head sticks up from the body.

4. Cut two eyes from the black construction paper. Glue the eyes to the head of the duck.

5. Fold the orange construction paper in half. Cut a duck bill on the fold so that you have a top and bottom bill that opens and shuts. Glue just the bottom half of the bill to the head of the duck, so that the top half can flop open.

6. Cut two legs with webbed feet for the duck from the orange construction paper. Glue the tops of the two legs to the bottom back of the duck so that the legs and feet hang down in the front of the duck.

Put your hands through the holes in the duck body and flap them like wings.

Quack, quack!

13

Ee is for . . .

Enormous Elephant

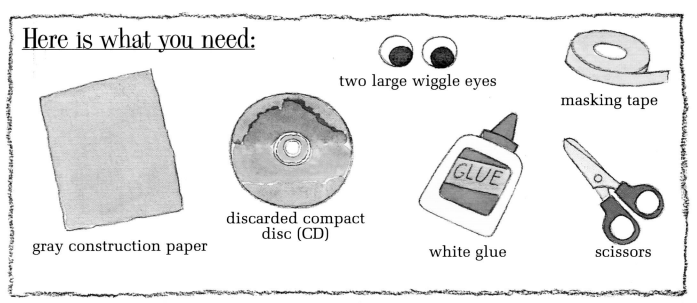

Here is what you need:

gray construction paper

discarded compact disc (CD)

two large wiggle eyes

white glue

masking tape

scissors

Here is what you do:

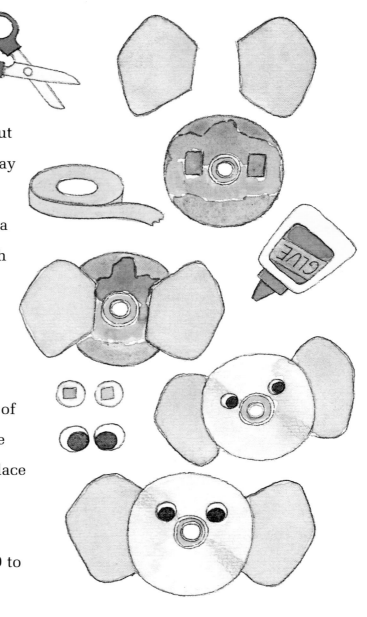

1. The CD will be the head of the elephant and you will put your finger through the hole to make the long nose. Cut two large ears for the elephant from the gray paper. Put a piece of masking tape on the back edge of each side of the CD to create a better gluing surface. Glue the edge of each ear over the masking tape so that the ears stick out on each side of the CD.

2. Put a piece of masking tape on the back of each eye and a piece on each side of the top of the nose hole. This will help the eyes to stick to the CD. Glue the eyes in place over the masking tape pieces.

Put your finger through the hole in the CD to give the elephant a long, wiggly nose.

Enormous!

Ff is for ...

Frog Friends Pin

Here is what you need:

two old puzzle pieces

white glue

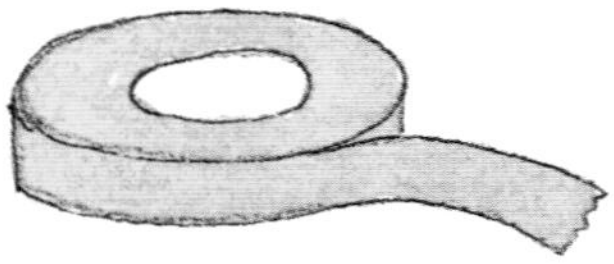

masking tape

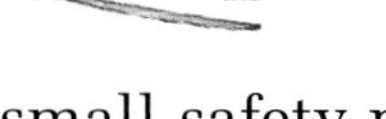

four small wiggle eyes

small safety pin

green and black markers

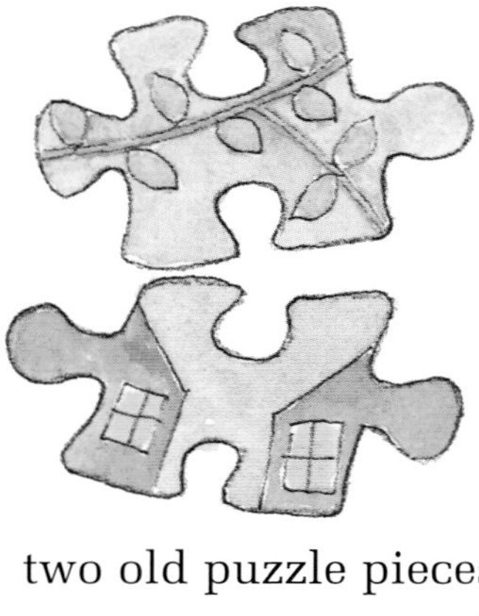

Here is what you do:

1. Choose two puzzle pieces that have a circle sticking out of two opposite sides and indentations on the other two sides. Color the back of both puzzle pieces green for the two frogs.

2. Turn the pieces so that the circles are the hands of the two friends. Glue two wiggle eyes to the top of each piece. Use the black marker to draw a mouth under the eyes on each piece.

3. Glue the two pieces together to look like they are holding hands.

4. Glue a safety pin to the back of the pieces. Use a strip of masking tape to hold it in place while the glue is drying.

Ribbit! Ribbit!

17

Gg is for . . .

Growing Green Grass

Here is what you need:

cereal-box
cardboard

piece of rickrack

ruler

stapler

1/2-inch (1-cm)
round stickers

black marker

green, blue, and skin-tone
construction paper

white glue

scissors

piece of brown pipe cleaner

Here is what you do:

1. Cut a 9- by 12-inch (23-by 30-cm) piece of cardboard from the cereal box. Glue a 9-by 12-inch (23-by 30-cm) sheet of blue paper over the cardboard.

2. Fold a sheet of 12- by 18-inch (30-by 46-cm) green paper in half lengthwise. Cut fringe all the way across the open end of the paper to make grass. Do not cut through the fold. Cut the strip of grass in half.

3. Staple the two sides of one of the strips of grass to the bottom of the blue paper.

4. Cut a 12-inch (30-cm) strip of blue paper. Staple one end of the strip behind the bottom of each side of the second strip of grass. Slide the second strip of grass down over the top of the blue paper, with the band behind the paper and the grass partway down behind the first strip of grass that is attached to the bottom of the blue paper.

5. Use the black marker to decorate some of the stickers to look like bugs. Stick the bugs in the grass.

6. Bend the piece of brown pipe cleaner to look like a worm and glue it in the grass. Cut a piece of rickrack for a caterpillar. Give it a face at one end with the black marker. Glue the caterpillar in the grass, too.

7. Cut two feet from the skin-tone paper. Make the leg portion long enough to reach the top of the blue paper. Draw toes on the feet with the black marker. Glue the two feet to the blue paper with the bottoms behind the top row of grass. Trim the legs off at the top of the paper.

To make the "green grass grow" just slide the band at the back of the paper up so that the grass gets higher.

Grow, grass, grow!

19

Hh is for . . .

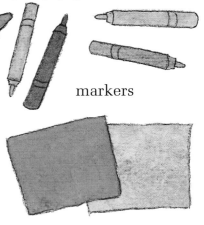

High-House Hat

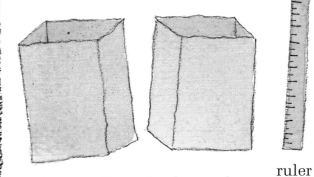

Here is what you need:

white glue

markers

two medium-size brown bags

ruler

scissors

colorful construction paper

20

Here is what you do:

1. Turn one of the bags upside down for the house. Draw the three sides of a door about 3 inches (8 cm) up from the rim. Cut the door, leaving the side uncut so that it will open and close.

2. Draw various-size windows around the bag house. Cut some of the windows out. For the rest, make shutters that open and close over the window by cutting the top and the bottom of the window then cutting up the middle. The two sides of the window will then open and close like the door.

3. Use the markers to color the door, window frames, and shutters. You might want to add shrubbery across the front of the house and window boxes under some of the windows.

4. Open the second bag and put it inside the house bag. Draw window details for the open windows on the second bag. Open the door and the shutters and draw behind them. You could make furniture that might be inside the house or people or pets.

5. Roll a 1-inch (2.5-cm) cuff on the rim of the bag house. Roll it again to secure the brim.

6. Fold a 9- by 12-inch (23- by 30-cm) sheet of construction paper in half widthwise to make a roof for the house. Glue the roof to the top of the house. Cut a chimney from construction paper to glue on one side of the roof.

You might want to add other details to the house such as a bit of fiberfill coming out the chimney for smoke, a photo of you behind the door, or pictures of flowers and furniture cut from magazines or catalogs. The windows can be bordered with trim or thin ribbon, and a bead would make a very nice doorknob.

Have fun designing your own High~House Hat !

Ii is for . . .

Icy Ice Skates

Here is what you need:

scissors

plastic
disposable cup

aluminum foil

water

plastic doll friend

Here is what you do:

1. Tear off a square of foil. Fold it in half to strengthen it. Mold the foil over the top of the cup. Use the scissors to poke a hole in the center of the foil. Remove the foil and set aside.

2. Fill the cup about half full of water. Put the foil back over the top of the cup. Stick the legs of the doll friend down through the hole in the cup so that it stands in the center of the water, supported by the foil.

3. Put the cup of water and the doll in the freezer until the water is completely frozen.

4. Run the outside of the cup under warm water for a few seconds to loosen the ice enough to pop it out of the cup.

Now your doll friend has icy ice skates! Slide the doll around on a waterproof floor. Make more than one skating doll friend and you can have a race. These are very fast skates!

Incredible!

23

J j is for . . .

Jump Up Jack-in-the-Box

Here is what you need:

ruler

old sock

craft feather

red felt

stickers

square tissue box

white glue

markers

construction paper

stapler

scissors

24

Here is what you do:

1. Cut around three sides of the bottom of the tissue box to make a door for the box that will open and close. Cut a piece of construction paper and glue it over the top of the door to cover the print that is on the bottom of most tissue boxes. Color the inside of the door with a marker. Decorate the sides and top of the box with stickers.

2. Measure 10 inches (25 cm) from the toe of the sock and cut off the rest, leaving a 10-inch (25-cm) long sock with toe as the body of the puppet. Cut a triangle-shaped hat from the red felt. Glue the hat to the front of the toe of the sock. Glue the craft feather on one side of the hat to decorate it.

3. Use the markers to give the puppet a face.

4. Cut a 2-inch (5-cm) slit up each side of the open end of the sock. Staple the two sides of the sock on each side of the opening in the tissue box, with the puppet inside the box.

To use the puppet put your hand inside the puppet and curl it up inside the box. Push your hand up and open it to make Jack pop out of the box.

Boing~ Boing!

Kk is for . . .

Kangaroo's Kid

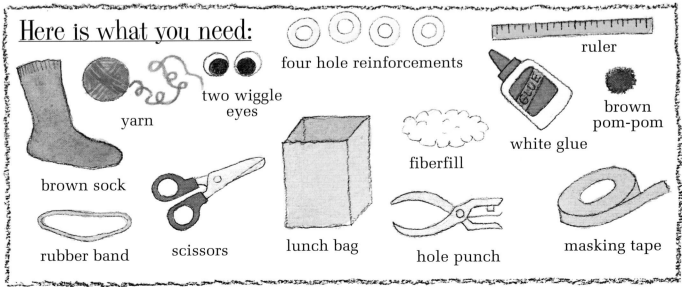

Here is what you need:

four hole reinforcements

ruler

yarn

two wiggle eyes

brown sock

fiberfill

white glue

brown pom-pom

rubber band

scissors

lunch bag

hole punch

masking tape

Here is what you do:

1. Fold the top of the lunch bag down three times to make a pocket for the baby kangaroo. Punch a hole in each side of the bag. Put a hole reinforcement on each side of the two holes to strengthen them. Cut a 30-inch (76-cm) length of yarn. Tie each end of the yarn through the hole on each side of the bag.

2. Stuff the toe of the sock with fiberfill to form the head of the kangaroo. Put the rubber band around the sock below the fiberfill to make the neck. Stuff the rest of the foot of the sock with fiberfill, then knot off the end. Cut off the excess sock.

3. Put a piece of masking tape on the back of each eye to create a better gluing surface. Glue the two eyes to the top portion of the toe of the sock. Cut a pointed snout from the extra sock piece and glue it on the face below the eyes. Glue the brown pom-pom to the end of the snout for a nose.

4. Cut two arms and two ears for the kangaroo from the extra sock piece. Glue the arms on the front of the kangaroo, and glue the ears on top of the head.

A baby kangaroo is not really called a kid. It is called a joey. Hang the bag around your neck for a kangaroo pouch. Put the joey in the pouch and go for a hop.

Hop! Hop! Hop!

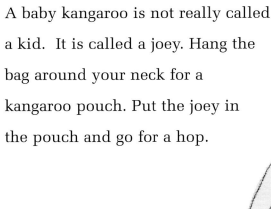

27

L l is for . . .

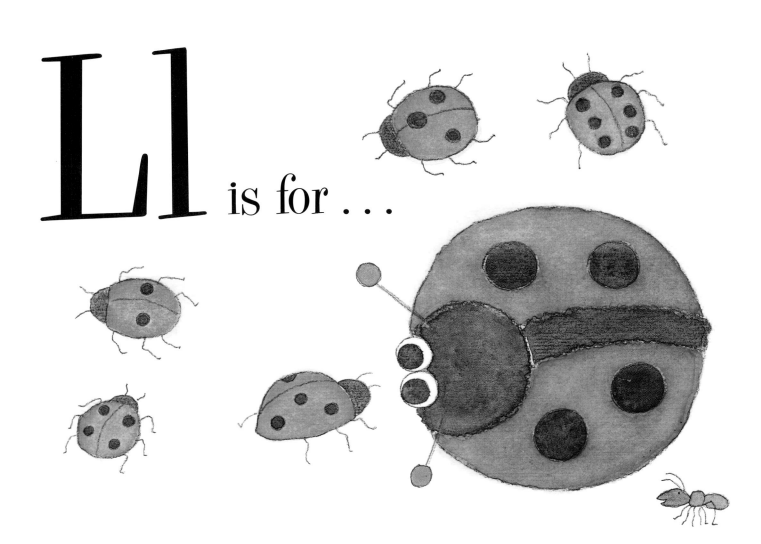

Lucky Little Ladybug

Here is what you need:

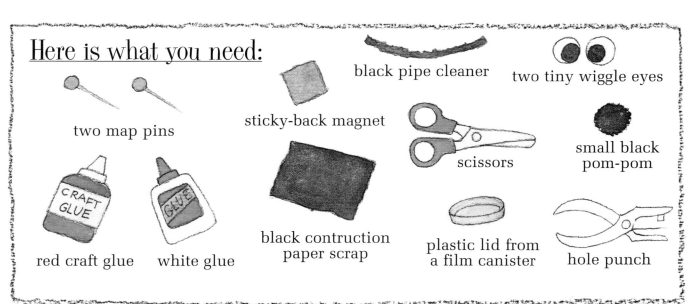

two map pins

sticky-back magnet

black pipe cleaner

two tiny wiggle eyes

scissors

small black pom-pom

red craft glue

white glue

black contruction paper scrap

plastic lid from a film canister

hole punch

Here is what you do:

1. Fill the inner rim of the plastic lid with red glue for the body of the lady-bug. Cut a piece of black pipe cleaner to fit exactly across the glue circle. Set it in the glue. Punch four holes from the black paper. Put two on each side of the pipe cleaner for the ladybug's spots. Use the white glue to attach the black pom-pom on one end of the pipe cleaner for the head. Let the glue dry for several days.

2. When the glue seems almost dry carefully pry the ladybug out of the lid. It might still be wet under the dried glue. Loosen the bug to let the air get underneath and let it dry completely on the plastic lid.

3. Glue two tiny wiggle eyes to the head of the ladybug. Dip the ends of the two map pins in glue and push them into the top of the head for the antennae.

4. Put a piece of sticky-back magnet on the bottom of the ladybug.

This bug would like to crawl up your refrigerator.

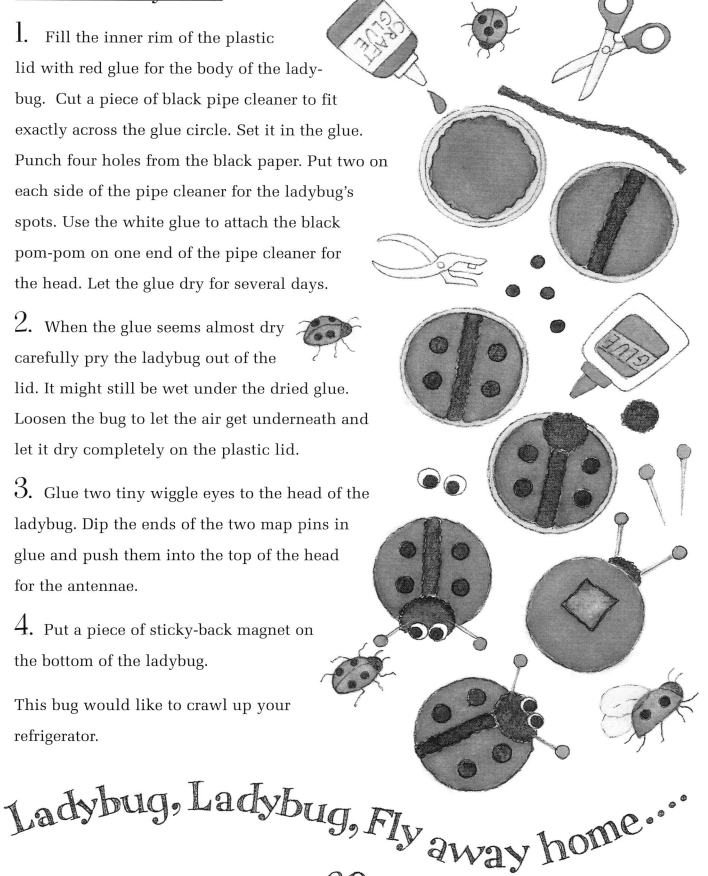

Ladybug, Ladybug, Fly away home....

29

M m is for ...

Most Marvelous Moose

Here is what you need:

black, brown, tan, and white
construction paper scraps

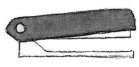

scissors

stapler

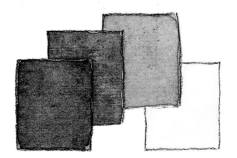

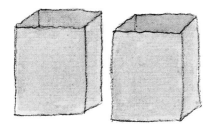

two brown lunch bags

white glue

30

Here is what you do:

1. Cut off the top third of one of the lunch bags. Crumple the top part of the bag that you cut off and put it into the bottom of the bag for stuffing. Glue the opening of the stuffed bag shut, leaving the bottom part puffed out. This will form the nose and muzzle of the moose.

2. The bottom of the second bag will be the top of the moose's head. The folded-over bottom of the bag will be his brow. Glue the glued closed end of the muzzle halfway down the second bag, then staple the two sides of the muzzle to the bag. It should now hang down off the front of the face.

3. Cut two nostrils for the moose from the black paper. Glue them to the flat bag bottom at the end of the muzzle.

4. Cut circle eyes from the white paper and smaller circle pupils from the black paper. Glue the pupils to the center of the white eyes, then glue the eyes to the face so that the tops are slightly under the brow of the moose.

5. Cut two ears from the brown paper. Glue an ear under each side of the brow.

6. Cut two large antlers from the tan paper. Glue the ends on each side of the back of the moose head so that the antlers stick out on each side of the head.

Maybe this moose likes muffins!

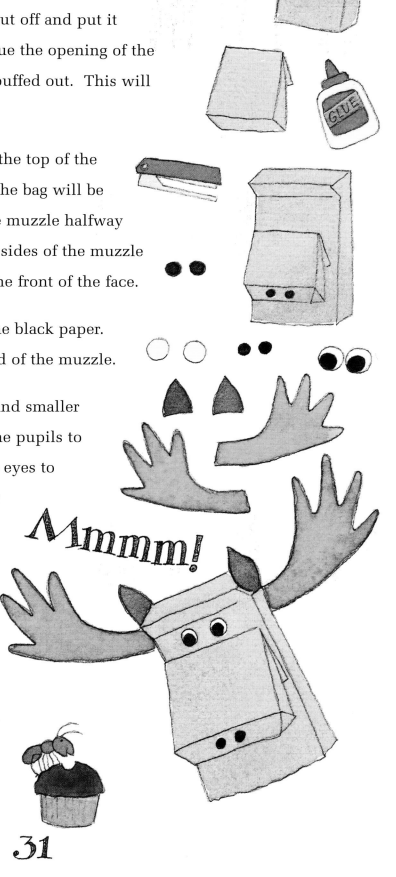

Mmmm!

31

N n is for . . .

Nice New Nose

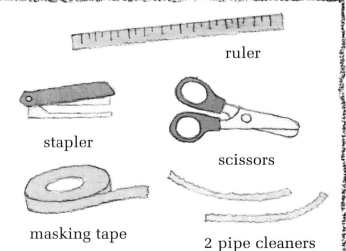

Here is what you need:

red and black
construction
paper

old panty hose

stapler

masking tape

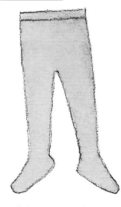

ruler

scissors

2 pipe cleaners

Here is what you do:

1. Cut a red triangle with 4-inch (10-cm) sides from the red paper. Round off the edges to make it look like a large nose. Fold the nose and staple the fold as close to the edge as possible and toward the top to hold it in a three-dimensional nose shape.

2. Cut a 5-inch (13-cm)-wide mustache from the black paper. Use the masking tape to attach the top of the mustache to the back of the bottom of the nose.

3. Shape the end of each of the pipe cleaners into a 3-inch (8-cm) circle to make the two sides of the eyeglasses and join the two circles together.

4. Cut the waistband off the panty hose. Staple the top of the nose to the inside of the waistband. Staple the glasses over the bridge of the nose. Cover any staple ends inside the band with masking tape.

New Nose!

You now have a very nice new nose to wear. Slip the waistband over your head so that the glasses are in front of your eyes and the new nose covers up your own nose.

33

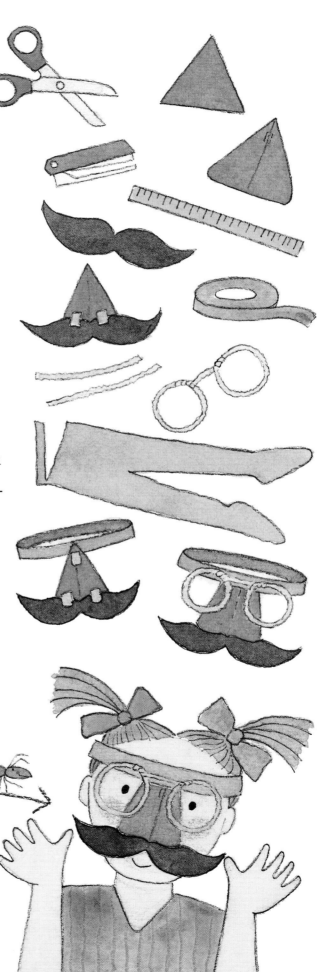

Oo is for . . .

Oval Owl

Here is what you need:

stapler

scissors

white glue

two craft feathers

ruler

yellow, white, and black
construction paper

oval-shaped
shoulder pad

12-inch (30-cm) orange pipe cleaner

Here is what you do:

1. Cut two 2-inch (5-cm) circles from the white paper for eyes. Cut two slightly smaller circles from the yellow paper and glue them to the center of the white circles. Cut two even smaller black circles for the pupils and glue them in the center of the yellow circles.

2. Turn the shoulder pad pointed end down. This will be the body of the owl. Glue the eyes to the top of the pad.

3. Cut a triangle-shaped beak from the yellow paper. Glue the beak on the owl below the eyes.

4. Glue a craft feather on each side of the body for wings.

5. Cut two 1-inch (2.5-cm) pieces from the orange pipe cleaner. Wrap a piece around each end of the long piece of pipe cleaner to form the toes. Bend the pipe cleaner in half to make the two legs with feet on the ends. Staple the fold of the pipe cleaner to the back of the bottom of the owl.

Whooo . . . .

If you want this oval owl to be a puppet, staple the top and sides of a second shoulder pad to the back of the owl.

Pp is for . . .

Pear Print Penguins

Here is what you need:

salt

Styrofoam tray

white glue

6 wiggle eyes

black poster paint

white and orange
construction paper

newspaper
to work on

1/2 of a pear

scissors

craft stick

fiberfill

Here is what you do:

1. Pour some of the black poster paint on the Styrofoam tray. Push the craft stick through the outside of the pear half to make a handle. Dip the pear into the black paint and print a pear shape on the paper. Print three pear shapes for the bodies of three penguins.

2. Cut a triangle-shaped beak and two feet for each penguin from the orange paper. Glue the beak to the top section of the penguin and the feet on the bottom. Glue two wiggle eyes above each beak.

3. Glue a puff of fiberfill to the center of each penguin to make a white tummy.

4. Spread glue around the bottom portion of the penguins and shake salt over the glue for icy snow.

You might want to use watercolors to paint some pretty colors in the sky behind the penguins to look like the northern lights.

Perfect!

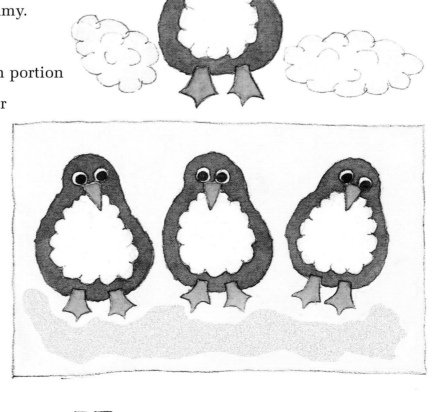

37

Qq is for . . .

Queen of Heart's Quilt

Here is what you need:

four or more zip-to-close bags

red tissue paper or red napkins

stapler

old valentines

paper and doily hearts

fiberfill

38

Here is what you do:

1. Each zip-to-close bag will be a section of the quilt. You can make the quilt with four or more bags. Fill half the bags with fiberfill as the background. Put in a pretty paper heart or valentine in front of the fiberfill. Close the bags.

2. Fill the remaining bags with crumpled red tissue paper or red napkins as the background. Put a pretty paper heart or valentine in each of these bags, too. Close the bags.

3. Staple the sides of a white and a red bag together. Staple the top of the remaining red bag to the bottom of the white bag and the top of the remaining white bag to the bottom of the red bag. Staple together the sides of the two bottom bags that are touching.

Quite cozy!

You can make the quilt larger by adding more bags. You might have some ideas for different things to put in the quilt bags for decoration.

Rr is for . . .

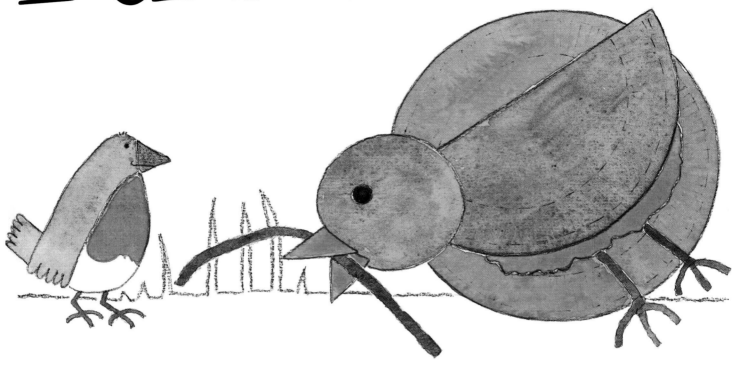

Red, Red Robin

Here is what you need:

red tissue paper

ruler

brown, black, and orange construction paper

brown and green poster paint and paintbrush

NEWS
newspaper to work on

12-inch (30-cm) brown pipe cleaner

Styrofoam egg carton for drying

two 9-inch (23-cm) uncoated paper plates

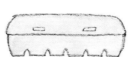
white glue

scissors

stapler

paper fastener

Here is what you do:

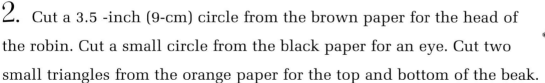

1. Paint the top of one paper plate green. Paint the second paper plate brown on one side. Turn it over and paint only the rim of the other side brown. Put it on a Styrofoam egg carton to dry.

2. Cut a 3.5 -inch (9-cm) circle from the brown paper for the head of the robin. Cut a small circle from the black paper for an eye. Cut two small triangles from the orange paper for the top and bottom of the beak.

3. The head will be sideways. Glue the eye to the top middle portion of the brown circle head. Glue the two triangles to one side of the head, with the bases overlapped, but the top points apart to look like an open beak. Cut a 5-inch (13-cm) piece of brown pipe cleaner. Glue it in the beak of the bird to look like a worm.

4. Fold the brown plate in half with the painted rim on the inside. Staple the two sides of the folded plate together. Push a paper fastener through the top back portion of the back side of the bird, then push the fastener through the green plate to attach.

5. Fold the remaining piece of pipe cleaner in half to make legs for the bird. Cut a 1-inch (2.5-cm) piece off each end of the legs. Wrap a piece around the bottom portion of each leg to make feet. Staple the top folds of the legs inside the bottom of the bird so that the legs hang down.

6. Crumple a 12-inch (30-cm) square of red tissue paper for the red breast of the robin. Rub glue over the inside of the folded body, then stuff the tissue up in between the two sides of the bird. Bob the robin up and down on the green grass by rocking it back and forth on the paper fastener.

Tweet!

Ss is for . . .

Seed With a Secret

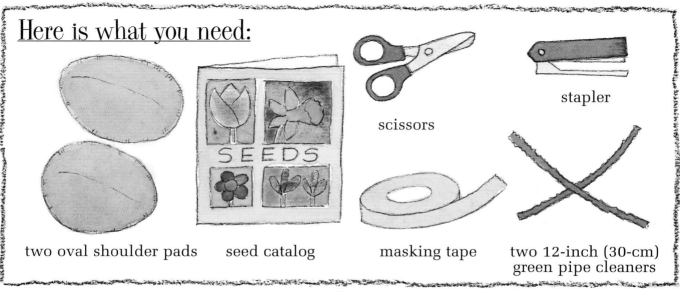

Here is what you need:

two oval shoulder pads   seed catalog   scissors   stapler   masking tape   two 12-inch (30-cm) green pipe cleaners

Here is what you do:

1. Hold the two shoulder pads together with the top sides on the outside. Staple the two shoulder pads together across one long side. Turn the pads so that the point is at one side with the bottom closed and the top open. This will be the seed.

2. One green pipe cleaner will be the stem of the flower. Wrap the second pipe cleaner around the first, and then shape the two ends into leaves. Trim off any extra pipe cleaner you don't need.

3. Find a picture of a big flower in the seed catalog. Cut the head of the flower out. Staple the flower to the top of the stem. Cover the staples at the back of the flower with masking tape to keep them from catching on the fabric of the shoulder pad.

4. Staple the end of the flower stem down in the bottom stapled seam of the seed. Curl the flower up to tuck it inside the opening of the seed.

It's your secret!

To show the seed's "secret" just reach in and uncurl the flower that is hidden inside.

Tt is for . . .

Tiny Turkey

Here is what you need:

pipe cleaners in
six different colors

orange chenille-bump
pipe cleaner

1-inch (2.5-cm)
colored wooden bead

ruler

white glue

two tiny wiggle eyes

black yarn

scissors

Here is what you do:

1. Cut a 2-foot (61-cm) length of black yarn. String the bead onto the yarn and tie the two ends together to make a necklace.

2. Thread the orange chenille-bump pipe cleaner halfway through the bead. Bend one end up to form the neck of the turkey, then bend the end down to shape the head. Bend the other end up to make a tail feather.

3. Cut six 1-inch (2.5-cm) pieces of pipe cleaner in different colors. Dip the end of each piece in glue and put it in the hole of the bead to make a tail feather. Bend all the tail feathers up.

4. Glue two tiny wiggle eyes to the head of the turkey.

Hang the tiny turkey around your neck and take it for a walk.

Gobble, Gobble!

45

Uu is for . . .

Under an Umbrella

Here is what you need:

silver tinsel

pipe cleaner

scissors

uncoated 9-inch (23-cm) paper plate

ruler

white glue

12- by 18-inch (30- by 46-cm) sheet of blue construction paper

black, yellow, and skin-tone construction paper

sticker stars

fiberfill

markers

46

Here is what you do:

1. Cut 3 to 4 inches (8 to 10 cm) off one side of the plate. Scallop the cut edge to look like the bottom of an umbrella. Color the umbrella with markers. Decorate the umbrella with sticker stars. Cut a 1-inch (2.5-cm) piece of pipe cleaner. Glue the piece to the top of the umbrella. Fold the remaining pipe cleaner into a curve on one end. Glue the other end behind the bottom of the umbrella to hang down to form the handle.

2. Cut a triangle shape from the yellow paper that is about 8 inches (20 cm) across the bottom and 10 inches (25 cm) on each side. Glue the triangle to the blue paper for the raincoat of the person. Cut a smaller yellow triangle for the sleeve. Cut a hand shape from the skin-tone paper. Glue the top of the hand behind the wide end of the triangle sleeve so that it sticks out. Glue the sleeve to the yellow raincoat.

3. Cut two black boots from the black paper. Glue the top of each boot under the bottom of the raincoat.

4. Glue the umbrella over the top part of the raincoat with the handle touching the hand of the person.

5. Glue fiberfill across the top of the paper for clouds.

6. Glue the silver tinsel hanging down from the clouds and on the ground to look like rain. If you do not have any silver tinsel for rain you can cut thin strips of aluminum foil to use.

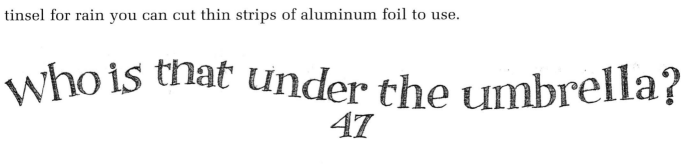

who is that under the umbrella?

47

V v 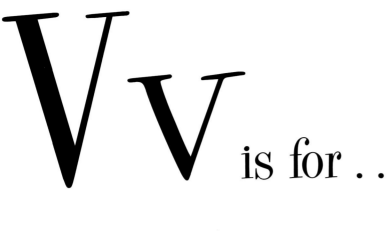 is for . . .

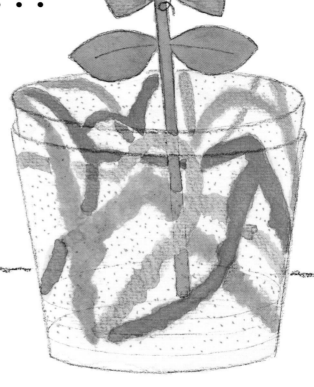

Very Pretty Vase

Here is what you need:

two identical disposable plastic cups

two or more colors of craft glue

glitter

Styrofoam tray to work on

Here is what you do:

1. Turn one of the cups upside down. Drizzle the bottom and sides of the cup with different colors of glue.

2. Sprinkle the glue with glitter.

3. Slide the second cup down over the first so that the glue is between the cups. Turn the cups over and leave on the Styrofoam tray to dry. This can take several days.

4. If the glue seems to be sliding down in the cup turn the cup over every day or two until the glue has dried. This will help keep the glue more evenly distributed. No matter where the glue ends up in between the two cups, this project looks very pretty.

This vase is best used with artificial flowers. If you get water between the cups the glue may dissolve and wash away.

Very Pretty!

W w is for . . .

Wacky Watermelon Necklace

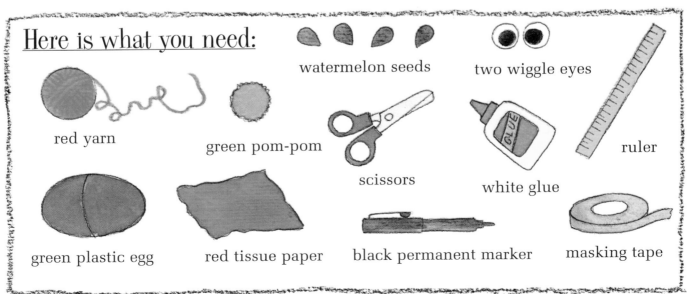

Here is what you need:

watermelon seeds

two wiggle eyes

red yarn

green pom-pom

scissors

white glue

ruler

green plastic egg

red tissue paper

black permanent marker

masking tape

Here is what you do:

1. If you do not have a green plastic egg ask a grown-up to spray paint green an egg of another color for you. Snap the green egg together. Use the black marker to draw lines from top to bottom all the way around the egg to make it look like a watermelon.

2. Make a hinge between the top and the bottom of the egg using masking tape.

3. Put strips of masking tape inside both the top and bottom piece of the egg to create a better gluing surface. Cut two 3-inch (8-cm)-square pieces of red tissue paper. Crumple each piece and glue it into one of the egg halves for the fruit inside the watermelon. Glue watermelon seeds on top of the red paper in each half.

4. Put a square of masking tape on the front of the top half just above the edge. Glue on the two wiggle eyes and the green pom-pom nose to make a face for the watermelon. (I told you it was a "wacky watermelon"!)

5. Cut a 2-foot (61-cm) length of red yarn. Tie the yarn to the hinge of the watermelon, then tie the two ends together to make a necklace.

Maybe you can make the wacky watermelon recite some other words that start with Ww.

Xx is for . . .

X-ray Vest

Here is what you need:

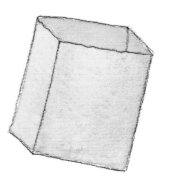

brown grocery bag

white and red
construction paper

ruler

white glue

scissors

Here is what you do:

1. Cut down the seam of the brown bag and cut around the bottom to remove it. Open the long strip of brown paper and fold it in half lengthwise. Cut a rounded piece out of the center of the fold about 6 inches (15 cm) long. Cut a 6-inch (15-cm) slit down the center of one side of the bag. Make sure you can now get your head through the hole in the bag to wear it with the slit side in the back.

2. Cut at least eight 1-inch (2.5-cm)-wide strips from the white paper that are about 5 inches (13 cm) long. These will be the ribs.

3. Cut a heart shape from the red paper about the size of your fist.

4. Glue the heart to the top center area of the front of the bag vest. Glue the white paper ribs down each side of the vest.

Do you know how many ribs you really have?

Yy is for ...

Yawning Yellow-Haired Puppet

Here is what you need:

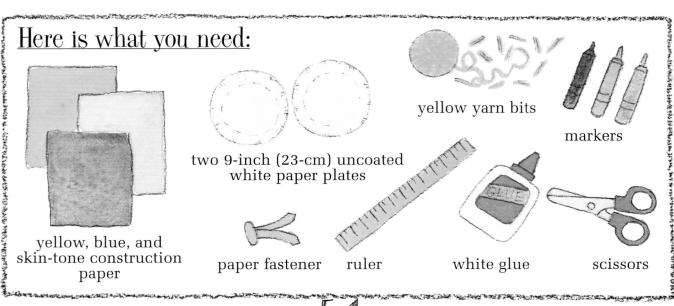

yellow, blue, and skin-tone construction paper

two 9-inch (23-cm) uncoated white paper plates

paper fastener

ruler

yellow yarn bits

markers

white glue

scissors

Here is what you do:

1. Cut two 1-inch (2.5-cm) holes out of one plate for the eyes. Cut a 1.5-inch (4-cm) hole below the eyes for the mouth.

2. Attach the cut plate to the second plate, both with eating side down, putting the paper fastener in through the center of the two plates for a nose.

3. Use markers to draw cheeks and eyebrows on the top plate. Draw a closed mouth on the plate behind the mouth hole. Draw an open eye on the plate behind each eyehole.

4. Turn the back plate to hide the first eyes and mouth drawing. Draw an open mouth on the plate behind the mouth hole and closed eyes in the eyeholes to look like the puppet is yawning.

5. Glue yellow yarn bits on the head of the puppet for hair.

6. Cut a 4- by 12-inch (10- by 30-cm) strip of blue paper for arms for the puppet. Fold the strip at an angle in the middle and glue the top of the fold behind the head so the two ends hang down for arms.

7. Trace your hands on the skin-tone paper and cut the hand shapes out. Glue a hand to the end of each arm. Cut four 2- by 4-inch (5- by 10-cm) strips of yellow paper for the cuffs at the end of the sleeves. Glue a cuff to the front and the back of the end of each arm to cover up the top of the hands.

When your puppet yawns, fold one arm up so that the hand covers the mouth.

What good manners!

55

Zz is for . . .

Zipper-Bag Zoo Book

Here is what you need:

pipe cleaner

scissors

black permanent marker

stapler

pictures of zoo animals from magazines

ruler

plastic berry basket

hole punch

green and blue construction paper

four or more zip-to-close plastic bags

white glue

Here is what you do:

1. Cut a piece of construction paper to fit inside each bag in your book as a liner. Cut green for animals that live on land and blue for animals that like the water.

2. Glue a different zoo animal picture to each square of paper. Cut a strip of berry basket for a fence and staple it to the bottom of the page for animals like camels or elephants.

3. Slide each animal picture into a zip-to-close bag with the open end on the right side of the picture. For animals like monkeys and birds, use the marker to draw the bars of a cage down the front of the bag.

4. Punch a hole in the top left corner of each bag. Cut a 2-inch (5-cm) piece of pipe cleaner. Thread the pipe cleaner through the hole in each bag, then twist the ends together to hold the bags together in a book.

By holding the book together with a piece of pipe cleaner you can untwist the pipe cleaner any time you want to add more pages.

Beaded Letters

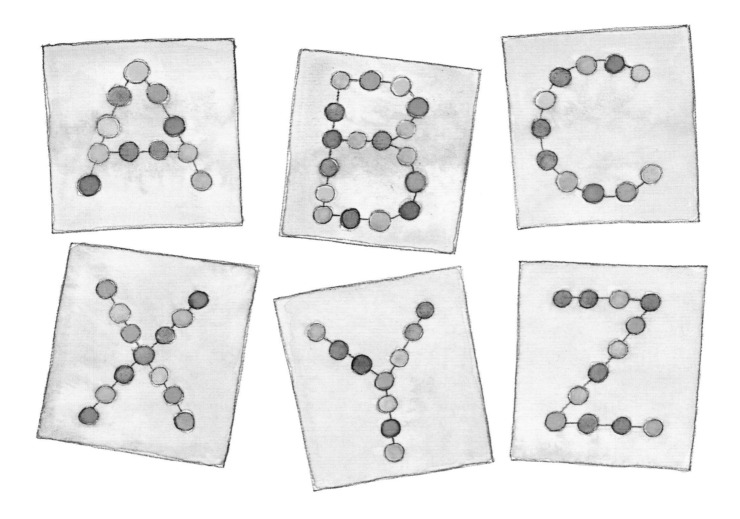

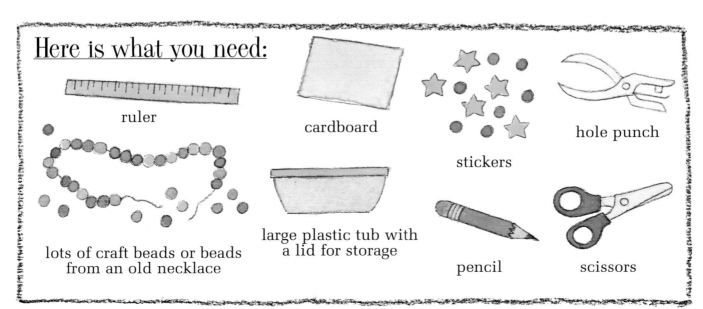

Here is what you need:

ruler

cardboard

stickers

hole punch

lots of craft beads or beads from an old necklace

large plastic tub with a lid for storage

pencil

scissors

Here is what you do:

1. Cut a 2- by 3-inch (5- by 8-cm) piece of cardboard for each letter of the alphabet.

2. Use the pencil to draw each letter on a piece of cut cardboard.

3. Punch holes in the cardboard along the lines of the letter.

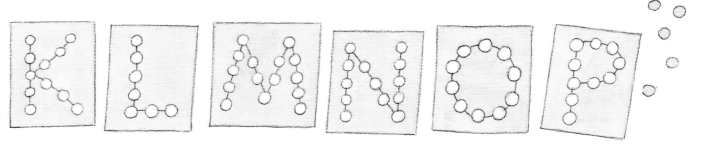

4. Make the shape of each letter in beads by putting a bead in each hole.

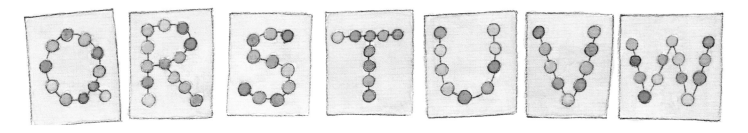

5. You can decorate your storage tub with stickers if you wish.

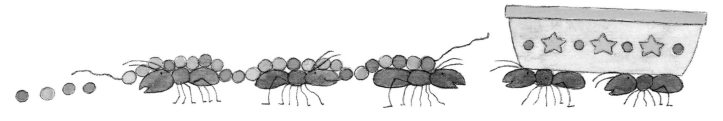

You might want to make other bead picture cards, too, such as shapes or numbers.

Rainbow Letter Pages

Here is what you need:

markers

scissors

sheet of paper for
each letter

old magazines

white glue

pencil

Here is what you do:

1. Draw or ask an adult to draw a capital and lowercase Aa on the top part of the paper. Make the letters into rainbow letters by going over them with lots of different color markers. This is fun and it is great practice for writing the letters.

2. Use the markers to draw some pictures of things that start with that letter on the page. You can also find pictures of things in magazines to cut out and glue on the page.

Make a page for each letter in the alphabet. Hang up each letter page as it is finished. When you have done all the letters, the pages can be tied together to make a book.

Magnetic Dots Letter Box

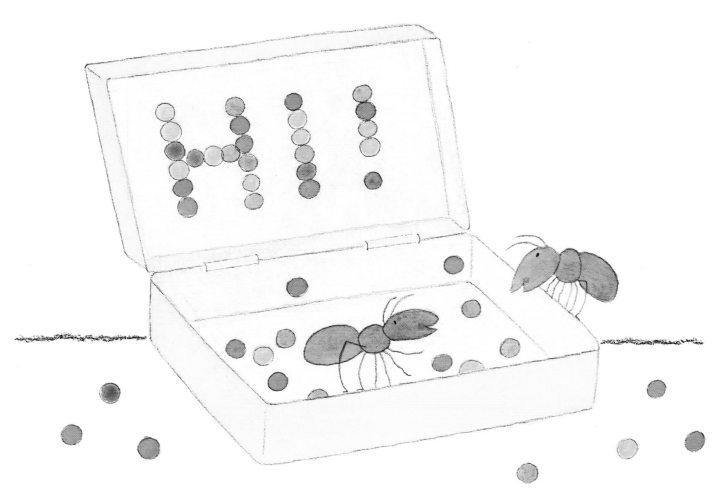

Here is what you need:

masking tape

sticky-back magnet strips

pencil

hole punch

markers

lots of construction paper scraps in different colors

metal box with hinged lid such as mints come in

white glue

scissors

About the Author and Illustrator

Twenty-five years as a teacher and director of nursery school programs have given Kathy Ross extensive experience in guiding young children through crafts projects. Among the more than thirty-five craft books she has written are CRAFTS FOR ALL SEASONS, MAKE YOURSELF A MONSTER, CRAFTS FROM YOUR FAVORITE FAIRY TALES, CRAFTS FROM YOUR FAVORITE CHILDREN'S SONGS, and the *Holiday Crafts for Kids* series.

Jan Barger, originally from Little Rock, Arkansas, now lives in Plumpton, East Sussex, England, with her husband and their cocker spaniel, Tosca. She has written and illustrated a number of children's books and is known for her gentle humor and warm, friendly characters. She also designs greeting cards, sings with the Brighton Festival Chorus, and plays piccolo with the Sinfonia of Arun.

Together, Kathy and Jan have written and illustrated the companion volume to this book, KATHY ROSS CRAFTS LETTER SHAPES, and they are at work on volumes on colors, object shapes, and numbers.

Here is what you do:

1. Stick construction paper to the back of a magnetic strip. Punch lots of holes from the strip. Save the colored dots in the metal tin. They will stick to the bottom and sides of the tin. Make lots of dots in many different colors.

2. Trace around the lid of the box on colored paper. Cut the tracing out. Cover the top of the box with strips of masking tape to create a better gluing surface. Glue the paper to the top of the box. Use markers to decorate the paper. You might want to write your name on the paper, too.

To use the magnetic dots, open the box. Shape letters with the dots by sticking them to the inside of the open lid of the box. You can make pictures, shapes, and numbers with your magnetic dots, too.

HAVE FUN!